I0076688

" When you speak with an Owner who has already sold their company, you'll find that transitioning a business is more like a marathon than a sprint." Eric Gilboord

MOVING FORWARD

GET THE TRIPLE EFFECT

Sell your business for
3 times more and 3 times faster.

Eric Gilboord

www.EricGilboord.com
www.WarrenBDC.com

Published by SOHO Marketing Inc.

ISBN: 978-0-9868932-4-7

Copyright 2016 SOHO Marketing Inc. Publishing

All rights reserved. No part of this work covered by the publisher's copyright may be reproduced or copied in any form or by any means without the written permission of the publisher.

Important Disclaimer:
This publication is sold with the understanding that the author is not responsible for the results of any actions taken on the basis of information in this work.

DEDICATION

This book is dedicated to the hundreds of people I have been fortunate enough to work with, to have enjoyed endless conversations with and to have learned from. Thank you for generously sharing your experiences, including both your successes and frustrations, while working with this often challenging target group of Boomer Aged Business Owners. I could not have written this book without you.

Also to the many BABOs who spoke openly with me. Thank you for freely sharing your fears, concerns, ambitions and ideas. You represent the lifeblood of our economy and this book. It has been written for you. Please take it to heart.

To my children and grandchildren who constantly inspire me to do more with my life and get more out of it. May you one day consider coming into our company as I prepare for my own transition.

Finally, to the love of my life Linda Lou. I really could not do what I do without your patience, understanding and encouragement. It is limitless and appreciated by me more than others may realize. But I know you do.

Eric, Dad, Papa Ricky

Contents

INTRODUCTION

Like Having A Bag Over Your Head

My thoughts, tips and recommendations in this book may not apply to everyone, but they are all valid and should be considered by any Owner hoping for a successful sale or transition of your company.

I've worked with hundreds of Owners of Small and Medium-sized businesses for over two decades. Some successful and others not so much. As an Owner of a few of my own companies I believe I've earned the right to comment on running a business and the inevitable selling, transitioning or closing of a company. Doesn't really matter what you call it. It still means you're no longer involved the way you used to be.

In the early days you tend to feel like the whole concept of running a company is overwhelming and some days it feels like running around with a bag over your head. Every day there are new challenges. A few steps forward, a few steps back. Some days are electrifying while others are humbling. But it got you up every day and kept you alive.

If you worked hard, the economy was with you and the industry you chose had legs you may have built a viable company, taken care of your family and put a little away for retirement.

Now you find yourself in the enviable, to some, or not so desirable position to others of being boomer age (that's you if you were born between 1946 and 1964) and facing a number of important decisions. What do I do with the business? Who could take over? Do I even want to sell? Where do I go for help? etc.

For many of you it can feel like you just put the bag back on and you're running around in the dark again.

Whatever you choose to do, this will be the most important decision you have ever made for the company, your family and yourself. Unfortunately, you're likely less prepared than you've ever been in your life for the choices ahead.

It's a gray world out there in the universe of buying and selling companies. Until recently the standard position of valued advisers was, it will take 5 years to get your company ready, find a suitor, put together a deal (that is if it didn't fall apart) and ease the transition for the new Owners to your staff, customers and suppliers. At least that was the party line.

Today you can construct a deal in many ways and with a variety of Buyers. Money upfront, later or both. Short time frame or long transition. Outright purchase or partnership. Earn out and or shares in the Buyers company. Partner or employee purchase. Partial sale. Competitor or strategic Buyer purchases you. Fund or individual Buyer acquires you. You continue to run the company with or without authority. You work under contract and have no final say.

Just remember there are no real shortcuts. For every shortcut you take, there is a price to pay. Don't be surprised if it ends up being about 5 years though. There will be loads of decisions to make. Many successful Owners have tripped and fallen during the selling process. While others have done well. Which one will you be?

Thinking About My Future, Are You?

Yes, I know it sounds like a confession is coming. The irony is not lost. I went on a wonderful holiday and spent a lot of time thinking about my writing over the years via blogs, online and offline articles and in newspapers and magazines. I've also had great experiences speaking to small, medium and large groups as well as many one on one conversations with several hundred business Owners over the last 22 years.

Public speaking and writing started out several years ago as a way for me to share interesting and hopefully valuable learning that I'd picked up along the way. Initially I spoke and wrote about marketing tips and tricks. Swung back and forth between personal motivation, practical business tips, and straight out selling my services. All the while appealing to pretty much anyone with a small or medium-sized business.

Over the past year or so I purposely transitioned my subject matter into a vehicle to speak almost solely with Boomer Aged Business Owners. To my surprise far fewer readers dropped out and I guess the interest was broader than I first thought. With boomers getting older and more folks becoming boomer age my audience has been consistently growing.

My intention is to continue providing worthwhile thinking and suggestions to improve your personal and professional lives. Pretty much all the conversations I have today are with Boomer Age Business Owners. Remember, if you are 50+ years old you are a boomer.

At the end of each conversation I have with BABOs, sometimes in email form, I am told the same thing over and over again. Thank you Eric, you've given us a lot to think about. You've opened our eyes up to many things we didn't know we had to deal with.

As a business Owner your personal and business lives, for years, have intersected from the time you woke up until you hit the pillow at night. It's unreasonable to think you could just switch off without some assistance. So making a decision to do just that is of great importance and not to be taken lightly. Those around you, family, friends, trusted advisers and business associates need to understand what you're going through. More importantly you need to understand what is happening to you.

So why am I writing this book? The answer is simple. There are far too many of you who are completely unprepared for what is coming. As each year goes by the problem grows nationally, globally and unquestionably in your own family and company.

The average age of a boomer in Canada and the United States is closer to the mid 60's. As you creep up on your late 60's or early 70's the decision to move forward and do something about your business will be made for you.

Poor health will affect either you, a spouse, a parent or a partner. The industry in which you operate is changing and you could find yourself on the wrong side of change. Competitors are coming and they are well funded, younger, smarter and stronger. That makes you really vulnerable.

So what does all this mean? You need to act now, not tomorrow. It's the night before exams and while some of you have prepared properly, the statistics are overwhelmingly against the remaining 90% who have not prepared and will inevitably struggle to transition their company. Or as some are seeing today, sell for pennies on the dollar or just give up and close the door.

At WarrenBDC our goal is to assist as many Owners and their families as we can, to move forward into the next fulfilling phase in their lives. And no, I do not mean travel and play golf for the duration. That gets old really quickly.

So I'm asking you to take that first step. Read this book, talk to those closest to you and move forward into your future. Yes it's more frightening than you can imagine and way more rewarding than you ever dreamed possible.

Let's Get Started

This book has been written specifically for Boomer Aged Business Owners. As a BABO you're likely going through a challenging time in your life. One of the biggest events you have to face today, as a Boomer Aged Business Owner, is to sell or transition out of your company. The first stumbling block is taking that first small step forward.

You've run the company your entire adult life or at least a good portion of it. The norm for you is a personal life that revolves around going into the office. Sometimes more often than you or your spouse like. When you're not at work you're thinking about the company. It's been a great ride filled with ups and downs. But you wouldn't have it any other way.

Realizing a successful sale or transition is key to your future. Many Owners are counting on the sale as all or part of their retirement plan. You will need money and I don't know anyone who really knows how much. So erring on the side of more is the better bet.

Many Owners don't know what they don't know. Even fewer of you have any sense as to what you'll do with the post Owner years. So consequently you may be the least prepared for the single largest sale you'll ever make.

Unfortunately, Owners are waiting far too long to take this step and your businesses are becoming less desirable to Buyers every day. You don't realize that no movement is the worst thing you can do. Not preparing for a sale will almost guarantee you a negative experience.

It's time to shed some light on transitioning out of your company. 'Moving Forward' was written as a wakeup call. A splash of cold water on your face. The end of the ride is coming and you better be prepared.

Owners need to clearly understand you are not alone. The 'selling' choices available to you are numerous and as varied as your individual needs.

I want to help you understand it's not a black or white choice of selling or not selling. There is in fact a huge gray area that sits between selling and 'dying with your boots on'. Your company may be worth X today the way it is. But by making some changes and improving the value of the business it could help you to sell for considerably more.

There is no question you will need help. A strong team of experienced outside professionals can take a challenging selling situation and turn it around. After all, if you could have done it yourself you would have already.

This book is about both the emotional and practical struggles Owners are having.

At the same time 'Moving Forward' will serve to help your family members and Buyers better understand these challenges from the Owner/Sellers' perspective.

Who Else Will Benefit From This Book?

In addition to BABOs, their families, and Buyers there are also many trusted advisers who will gain valuable insights. Their services in Law, Accounting, Wealth Management, Banking, Merger and Acquisition, Business Brokering, and more Coaches of all types than ever will be a great aid to the Owner going through transition.

A big challenge exists today among many advisers trying to understand and help their BABO clients. As a trusted adviser, you likely have clients stuck on agreeing whether or not it's time to start transitioning their company. You try talking to them but they don't listen.

Maybe you're a past Owner looking to help other Owners. Or you want to buy into a business or two yourself and dealing with other Owners has been a challenge. Hopefully you're one of the lucky few Owners who prepared in advance for the day you would exit your company and have already successfully transitioned.

Or possibly you're a business Owner who underestimated the complexities of selling their own company. Things didn't go quite as well as you hoped and now you're looking for a way to improve your current financial situation by coaching other Owners.

In any case, you're hoping to help Owners transition. Ideally, reading this book will give you some insights into the BABO and how to successfully work with them.

I Can't Write A Book More Important For You

This is NOT the definitive book of exits. On the contrary, it's written with the sole purpose of getting BABOs to move forward with their exit plans. One step at a time.

I have found the biggest challenge today for Boomer Aged Business Owners is in taking that first small step toward selling your company. You have questions but likely don't know where to turn for the answers. Realizing a successful sale or transition is key to your future. As hard as this is to believe you will not live forever. So you need an action plan.

The economy is not ready for the record number of business Owners who will just close up shop one day and put their employees out of work.

Imagine if you just close down your small business. What happens to your 20 employees? Now add vendors who rely on your business. They could be hurt. Some of your customers will migrate elsewhere. But, depending on your business, other customers may be quite tied into your company. Transitioning to a new supplier could be difficult for them.

A decision about your business could trigger negative results in your company as well as others. Let's be conservative and say 30 families will be adversely affected by your decision to close down.

If you follow the thinking and 9 other Owners do just what you are contemplating, 300 families could be hurt. Or 100 Owners impact 3000 families. If only 1,000 Owners, out of the millions of boomer Owners, did the same thing it could result in 30,000 families being hurt. Where is the loyal long serving 57 year old worker going to go if you close down? Or your family member who relies upon you for work.

If you don't prepare properly, the fallout will be far worse than you think:

1. Your spouse/family will be left to run or sell the business. Your spouse may be forced to work with your partner. That goes two ways. How would you like to be in the position of working with your partner's wife? Sobering thought isn't it.

2. Company value will drop dramatically because you are not there to run it. In many cases you are the business. Want to find out if that's true?

3. Your employees may end up out of work.

4. Customers are not quite as loyal as you think.

5. Competitors will be circling your customer list within minutes.

6. In case your big plan is to die with your boots on. Good luck. You will likely be leaving a legacy and a mess. They'll definitely be talking about you. Maybe just not in the way you hoped.

If you don't want this to happen you have 2 choices:

1. Sell now, knowing it will be significantly harder than you thought, and you will realize far less payment for the business. The terms of the sale may not be exactly what you were hoping for, or even close. You'll have little choice and be forced to be content with the deal however it turns out.

2. Start getting your business ready for a successful sale or transition and have the future you always thought you could have. Become a company desired by Buyers. Sell for the amount you wanted or possibly far more. Sell on your terms.

You can't properly do #1 or #2 without a plan and a team to implement it. It's really not much more complicated than that.

Recently, we've been seeing more activity on social media and experiencing an unusually high increase in both first visits and repeat visits to our corporate website for Warren Business Development Center Inc. www.WarrenBDC.com. We can link this to, trusted advisers directing their clients to us, some Owners slowly waking up, our own database mining and the power of social media.

You are not alone and the competition for finding a Buyer is just heating up. The sooner you get started, the more time you will have to increase the value of your business and the better your exit will be. It's a Seller's market, if you're ready.

4 Ideas For Boomer Aged Business Owners

I have many conversations today with Boomer Aged Business Owners (BABO) and or their trusted advisers. Here are some of the key ideas they thank me for sharing.

1. The first thought is that 80% of transitioning your company is about what is going on inside your own head. What you are thinking about, what's keeping you up at night, and the realization that you don't know what you don't know.

2. Secondly, the world of buying and selling companies is no longer black & white and solely transaction oriented, but many shades of gray. Old rules don't apply. You are a new unique generation of Owners. For many reasons your world and the challenges you face are not the same as the ones your parents dealt with when they were your age.

3. Thirdly, most BABOs don't know where to go for good, experienced, business transition specific, guidance and services. You don't know how much you need for retirement, no one does. If you think that's the only advice you need. Surprise!

4. If the first three are not enough, there's money out there. Buyers are looking for good companies to purchase. They're calling us, asking specifically for help finding, well prepared, quality businesses to purchase. And that is a hard item to find.

So what does all this mean? You need to act now, not tomorrow. Statistics are overwhelmingly against the 90% of you who have not prepared and will inevitably struggle to transition your company. It's not too late, you can still do well.

DIY Vs DIFY - Do It For You/With You

Why are some of you so hell bent on selling your company yourself? Typically with the help of your lawyer and accountant. But not professionals with business selling experience. Classic DIY vs DIFY. Eventually you will learn after getting your A** kicked a few times. Yes, you really do need experienced help. Experience in selling businesses!

Have you ever needed something done and it seemed like doing it yourself was quicker, easier and cheaper? Purging decades of collected stuff in the basement before selling your house. Took a little longer than you thought it would, but you got there. Doing your own taxes. How many possible deductions did you miss out on because you didn't know about the tax law changes? And the classic selling your home by yourself. There's a reason why real estate agents laugh when they see a FSBO (For Sale By Owner) sign on your lawn, and don't bother looking at your place.

Dealing with Sellers, inexperienced at selling a business, is typically time consuming and frustrating for Buyers. Usually it doesn't end well for either party.

The choice of DIY or find someone more qualified and or willing to DIFY is a daily occurrence. Some tasks seem ok to do on your own or while utilizing internal resources. i.e. nephew who knows everything about building websites, existing supplier who said they could make a new widget for you, employee who should be able to do it.

You're thinking, if it takes a little longer, comes out not quite 100% you can live with the results. After all you saved some money. Right?

Usually it takes way longer, costs much more in $ or frustration and never quite works the way you thought it would. As business Owners, we all have those experiences under our belt.

So why would you risk your single biggest asset to the same poor odds of success? Why would you try to sell your company without the benefit of an experienced team of professionals?

You may think you have the talent in place (lawyer, accountant, management), however you need to consider this. Unless they have real world experience buying and selling companies you may be asking them to do something they're not qualified to do. Are you really willing to take that chance with the single biggest sale you're likely ever to make? Yes I know, a little repetitious. But necessary!

And one more thing. You can't run a business and sell it at the same time. You need help, the experienced kind.

Are You Really Ready To Sell?

I attended a conference recently, focussed on business transition. The room was filled with Owners, experienced M&A folks, Business Brokers, Trusted Advisers and assorted other suppliers who provide many of the important skills required for a successful sale or transition.

The key takeaway was simply this. Most Owners, no matter how successful you are at making widgets, are woefully unqualified and under-prepared. You're just plain not ready to take on the serious, time sucking commitment of selling your business today.

There is so much to do and the facts are, most of you don't have the experience internally. Don't know what you don't know and will not be able to run the company successfully while getting ready or actually going through the process.

And it is a process. A long, detail oriented road to travel. Unfortunately, you may not ever arrive at your destination. Many Sellers have been left at the altar by the Buyer. Or oddly, you get nervous and become the runaway bride. Leaving the deal to die.

Here's What Can Get In The Way

1. The dream of many entrepreneurs and often times their spouse is to save the business for the kids. A few important questions first, before contemplating selling to your kids.

   Answer All These Questions

   a. Do they want to take over? Have you actually sat down with your children and asked?

   b. Are they old enough right now to have the conversation?

   c. Are they involved in the business today, either full or part time? Or even interested?

   d. Are they qualified to run the business today? Working in the business is very different from working on the business. Are they even qualified to do the job they have now in the company?

   e. Could they be qualified over time and with the right support? Can you afford to wait?

   f. Can they afford to buy the business? The fastest way to kill a business is to give it to someone. You've heard the joke. How do you make a $1,000,000 business? Give your kid a $3,000,000 company. Sad but true.

   g. What about the children who elect not to be involved? What do they get?

   h. There are so many more questions you will need to ask them and yourself.

2. Someone still has to run the business day to day. Unfortunately you have not planned for this. If you have a

larger company you may have staff to run the show for you. Typically if you have a smaller company, with under $3 million in annual sales the staff relies upon you for many of the day to day decisions and the business can stutter when you're not available.

3. You're overwhelmed by the process and don't have a qualified, experienced transition team in place. You think you have trusted advisers to help with the process but sooner than later you will discover they can't help you if they have little experience buying and selling businesses. I need to reinforce this!

4. Your partner has a different agenda and doesn't want to sell. Or at least not right now. Not for the price you think is reasonable. This is when you realize you and your partner have not had the heart to heart conversation you've been meaning to have and just how important it is. Get on it now!

5. In order to take advantage of the capital gains and other assorted exemptions, you need to have planned well in advance. In fact, there is so much wealth management planning you need to do, you should have started a few years ago. This financial planning and tax advice is about moving the proceeds from the sale of your business to your personal side. Only advisers with the proper experience can do this. We've all heard about the Owner who sold his company for $4 million and then wrote a cheque to the government for $2 million because he got the wrong tax advice. It happens all the time.

6. Your partnership agreement is out of date or nonexistent. Try getting an agreement where all partners are happy, after you've been working together for years. You will suddenly realize how different your respective views are on the business and life in general.

7. You've been taking money out of the business in various ways and that has to be normalized. In other words you have been using the business as your personal piggy bank and now you have to show your financials to prospective Buyers. They will be looking into every line of your reporting and will want to see the real story. No, you can't fool them!

8. Sales have been stagnant for too many years. Usually because you chose to stop growing. You were thinking, more sales means more work, more trouble and why bother when you're taking more than enough cash out of the business to pay for your lifestyle as it is. It may be catch up time!

9. There is no viable candidate internally to transition to. If there was, they would have raised their hand by now. Or maybe you just haven't been listening and someone terrific for the job is right in front of you. They may require some training, mentoring and management support but they do exist.

The list goes on and on. Makes you question whether selling even makes sense. Well here is one more sobering thought. Likely 80% of your wealth is wrapped up in the business. Kind of like having all your eggs in one basket. It's your move, what are you going to do?

10 Common Triggers For Selling A Business

As Rosanne Rosannadanna from SNL used to say. 'It's always something.'

1. You experience a negative event i.e. spouse, parent, partner or you get sick or dies.

2. Partner has finally come to you and said they want out. You weren't expecting this and now is not a good time for it to happen.

3. It's time for you to sell, but your partner does not want to. We all have different agendas.

4. The industry you operate in is changing and you are not prepared to change with it. Competition is on your tail and not letting up.

5. Your kids won't be taking over the business any time soon. Don't want the business, are unqualified to run it or can't afford to buy it.

6. You want to improve your life enjoyment i.e. time with family, spouse, travel.

7. You need the money from selling to finance your retirement, divorce, college for the kids or a medical situation. Or all of the above.

8. You're tired and not enjoying yourself any more.

9. Your spouse has finished working and wants to spend quality time with you.

10. You don't want to miss out on watching your grandchildren grow up. As some of you did with your own kids.

When You Don't Know What You Don't Know?

When we're unsure of ourselves, many of us go to extremes. We freeze up or boldly move forward unprepared. Only to make unnecessary mistakes. Anxiety builds and begins to affect other parts of our lives. Missed opportunities usually turn into regret. And regret can eat away at you like nothing else.

This is the case with transitioning. I'd like to suggest that you determine what you don't know about selling or transitioning your company and go out and get the answers. Sounds simple, but you are likely asking yourself, where do I start? And that's where it breaks down. It's one of the many reasons you're stuck.

Reading this book is a good start. Obviously the internet has answers. Maybe not the best resource but look for varying opinions and then make your own decisions. You will talk to some friends who have gone through the transition or maybe they are in the thick of it now.

But for real advice, what or who do you look for? Doesn't matter if it's finance, legal, strategy, operations, sales, marketing or people. There are experts in every field. Some are better than others and in a best world scenario you assemble a team made up of advisers who are very competent and comfortable for you to work with. They get you and whatever the specific task is becomes all pleasure and not pain. Ok maybe some discomfort, but that's life.

In my world, a consuming question colleagues keep asking is. Why are so many BABOs of established businesses stuck when it comes to selling your company?

I think one of the big reasons is because you don't know what you don't know. About the process. Your personal future, post sale. How much your company is worth and what a realistic price is. Who should be on your team. How much you should pay for help. What will happen to your employees. And the list goes on and on.

In fact, for many, this is the single largest sale you will ever make. Unfortunately the majority of you are ill prepared for this single key transaction.

And you don't know where to start. Confidentiality is important, skill sets are key and a combination of personal and business advice will be required.

Frankly I'm less concerned with where you go for help and much more interested in making sure you get going. As an incentive please understand, there are far more Buyers than Sellers currently. It's a Seller's market. But you have to be buy worthy.

Ask Yourself These Questions

1. Are you still trying to 'recover' the business value that you lost during the recession?

2. Do you really believe no one else can possibly run the business?

3. Would you rather keep all your eggs in one basket?

4. Are you concerned you don't know what to do with the money after selling? So you'd rather keep it invested in a known asset, your business.

Time To Start-Down

Over the last couple of years you've kicked some tires, read a few articles or books, spoke to a few friends and maybe some professionals with experience in selling businesses. Then you put it all on hold because selling your business was never a serious consideration. After all you were still young.

If you read the business press today, it is shocking the number of Boomer Aged Business Owners with no real plan to sell their business. In Canada it's estimated there are 550,000 Boomer Aged Business Owners.

1. Over 75% of you plan to sell within the next 10 years. That's a lot of competition.
2. Less than 10% of you have a team, formal exit or succession plan in place.
3. Over 82% expect the sale of your business to fund your retirement. That's a lot of pressure.

As I said earlier, over the years I've worked directly with hundreds of owners of small and medium-sized businesses, like yourself. And spoken with many more. It is disturbing to realize the number of entrepreneurs who don't have a real exit strategy in place. There is no thought out plan to sell or transition your business.

In addition there are a huge amount of business Owners willing to let your businesses go for well under what you could sell for. Mainly because you don't want to do the work to prepare the company for sale.

Or you've chosen to ride it out for a few more years, taking as much cash out of the business as you can and then plan to just close the doors with little or no thought for the negative impact on employees, vendors and customers. Let's not forget our economy which is not even close to being ready to absorb the impact of hundreds of thousands of Owners shutting down over a concentrated period of time.

The other option being considered by Owners is to 'die with your boots on'. These are the Owners planning to work until you drop. A plan based on loving what you do, working is an economic necessity or you simply don't know what else to do with your time. Or whatever story you want to tell yourself.

In many cases, initially, you're taking business selling advice from your current lawyers and accountants. Which is great if the trusted advisers have experience buying and selling companies. Not so good if they don't.

You are letting your baby go for 2, 3 or 4 x EBITDA* based on a volume of sales well below what it could be. Increased sales, a reshuffling of people, improved marketing, better operations and financial controls could all help to increase EBITDA* and therefore garner a sale price 6+ X. Especially when your annual sales break the magic $10,000,000 level. You could sell for far more than you have ever imagined was possible. It just requires some preparation.

*Commonly abbreviated as **EBITDA**, an accounting measure to calculate a company's net **E**arnings, **B**efore **I**nterest expenses, **T**axes, **D**epreciation and **A**mortization are subtracted. Used as a proxy for a company's current operating profitability.

You could wait a few years and receive much more for your business. Anything done to increase the value of the business will help to make the company more desirable to a Buyer and valuable to you the Owner.

For years you considered improvements to your marketing, operations, finance and sales departments. Thought about enhancing technology, or even replacing staff. But you never followed thru.

Every SMB I've ever visited always included the obligatory tour. The Owner inevitably introduced his staff as: This is Jeff our Marketing Manager but he's not really a marketing person more a sales guy. Meet Susie our Controller, but she's really only qualified as a bookkeeper. Jan who doesn't get along with anyone but I keep her anyway. And my children who couldn't get a job elsewhere so they work here, etc.

Always one step below what they should be. No not the whole staff or you wouldn't have a thriving business. Just a few key players who help to keep you back or cause some frustration. Well now you may want to reconsider. The new Owner will be assessing your people and your judgement in people. They will be spotted and quickly. It will be held against you.

There are good ideas not acted on because they were an unnecessary expense or it was so much work you just didn't bother.

If you have an established business, consider returning to why you got into the business in the first place. Get in touch with what you were passionate about and determine how to get back to doing the things that you can't wait to do each day.

There is no shortage of experienced folks to perform the functions you are not comfortable with or even qualified to do. Stop doing the stuff you hate and spend more time working on the business not in the business.

THE CURRENT MARKET

Are You Planning For The Future?

I do every day. That's not all, I also speak with advisers, update my thinking and accept mistakes as a valuable part of the learning process.

Taking the first step to resolve a problem or reach a goal is the fastest way to finish. The time it takes to fuss about it and worry is both counterproductive and emotionally draining.

You need to get some objective, fresh eyes thinking on what you could do with your company and your future.

Especially now when you should be investigating your options and making decisions about where you want to be and mapping out the route. If you don't know where you're going any road will take you there.

It's not only your future, but the well being of family, staff, customers and vendors you need to take into consideration.

Would Vs Could

The sad lament of the Owner who waited too long. The signs were there and all it took was recognition of the inevitable. And of course doing something about it.

I wish my staff would take over the company.
I wish my staff could take over the company.
Unfortunately, they are not ready or interested.

I wish my children would take over the company.
I wish my children could take over the company.
Unfortunately, they are not ready or interested.

I wish someone would buy my company.
I wish someone could buy my company.
Unfortunately, we are not ready and no one is interested.

I wish I would have sold my business sooner.
I wish I could have sold my business sooner.
Unfortunately, I was not ready or interested.

You Can't Do Both, Run And Sell A Business

Many have tried to simultaneously run their business and sell it at the same time. It usually ends in failure or at the very least an exhausting and confusing experience.

Look at it this way. For most owners, running their business is a full time job. A job you know well, one that you pretty much do on instinct fuelled by loads of experience. Your team has worked with you and each other for a reasonably long period of time. So decisions are made quickly. They are important and key to keeping the machine running smoothly. But they tend to revolve around you.

Selling a business is filled with unknowns. A process you're unfamiliar with. Add in new team members who you may not be comfortable with yet. There will be a requirement for decisions that you either don't have the experience with or the time to learn.

The questions, requests for documentation and meetings never end. Sleepless nights and a strain on your family life will add to the frustration. It's like taking on a new job or project for a customer. One you are currently very unqualified for. You will need to go through a learning curve that you likely have no time for.

So why add this additional and very difficult job to your usual busy schedule? It's a recipe for disaster, or at the very least failure. It will almost certainly adversely impact your company. Do you really want to do this as a second job?

You and your business need to be in a place where the company runs without you. This is a good thing. If you want the best shot at selling, a Buyer wants to see that the company can run smoothly without you anyway. One day you will no longer be in the picture. The Buyer needs to believe this is realistic.

This is one of the most important messages in my book. I can't emphasize this enough. This does not mean daily phone calls or emergency emails. Your company must run under any condition without you. No exceptions. The new owner will likely not have access to you and must be able to count on the staff in any situation.

Should I Stay Or Should I Go?

It's all about exploring options, making incredibly important decisions and moving yourself forward.

Whether you're a retiree or one of the many now falling into the category of BABO - Boomer Aged Business Owner, change is in the air. Tough decisions are being wrestled with by pretty much all of us and no one can know what is best for you other than you and the family, friends and business associates who have earned your trust.

Whatever you do, looking at all your options is your next smart move. Inevitably if you don't take control of your future, or at the very least explore your options, it will be decided for you. The universe is a strange and powerful place. When decisions are not made, or worse avoided, the vacuum tends to get filled. Power is taken from you and choices are then made for you. Not always good   ones.

Sometimes song lyrics can express our inner most feelings better than we can ourselves. One of the biggest issues keeping BABOs up at night is answering the question The Clash so eloquently stated in their hit song 'Should I stay or should I go?'. Go ahead try and get it out of your head now.

If you stretch your mind just a bit and listen to the lyrics as if you're talking to your business I think you'll see my point.

So take a quick break, head over to YouTube and play the song. Unfortunately I can't legally show the lyrics here.

And turn the volume up.

Current State Of The BABO World

1. Boomers own about 63% of private businesses in both Canada and the United States.

2. The majority or 80-90% of their wealth is tied up in their business.

3. More than three quarters or 76% plan to transition over the next 10 years. With almost half, 48% in the next 5 years. Sounds like it could be a bit crowded and competitive.

4. Typically, 12 months after selling 75% of Owners regret the decision. If you want to know how to avoid the whole regret part I suggest you keep reading. Have I got your interest?

5. Of the businesses available and put on the market, 70-80% don't sell.

6. Most, 85%, of family-owned businesses are first generation.

7. Less than 30% of family-owned businesses survive into the second generation.

8. Only 3% make it successfully into a third generation. That is a whopping 97% failure rate. Just because you took over from a previous generation and ran the company successfully, does not mean your kids will, want to or are qualified to.

9. A little over two thirds or 67% of boomer Owners are between 50 and 69 years old. Stop for a minute and take it in. Now continue.

10. Three quarters of you, 75%, have an annual company revenue of under $5 million.

11. A quarter of you, 24%, say you're familiar with the transition options available to you. Half or 44% aren't and a third, 32%

are not sure. That's a lot of Owners in the dark about their future.

12. Most, 88%, have NOT YET established a formal transition team. Sounding familiar?

13. Again most of you, 86%, have no formal education related to transitioning your business.

14. Three quarters of Owners, 67%, have no provisions in place if key personnel get ill or die.

15. Half of you, 50%, have no thoughts about what you'll do in your post transition life after the business is sold and you are completely out.

Wow that was a mouthful. Take another minute and let it sink in. I guarantee you one thing. You don't know what you don't know. That will absolutely lead to a whole lot of trouble. The challenge is to find the best advisers for you.

Here is just one example of the misguided thinking many of you are using today to make decisions and move forward.

You think if you keep the company for a few years longer and take as much cash as you can out, it will more than make up for what you think you could sell for today. Then, in a few years, you'll sell for whatever you can get or just close down the company and get on with your life.

Nice plan, unfortunately, putting off selling or even just getting the company ready for transition or 'dying with your boots on' are not really exit strategies, now are they?

What if, in the meantime, you get ill or worse? The mess you'll leave behind for family, partners, management, employees, customers and vendors will ensure they continue to talk about you for a very, very long time to come.

It's not all doom and gloom. There is a silver lining. What if you could delay selling, keep taking money out, increase the value of the company and sell for more later. More than you think you could get now, much more.

Have your cake and eat it too. Hmm, that is worth looking into.

As a successful business Owner, you're smart enough to at least consider all the options available to you. But where do you go to learn more about them?

The answer is, you search out experienced professionals with a track record of buying and selling companies.

It's Not Ok To Wait Any Longer

You can deny it all you want. But if you're a Boomer Aged Business Owner, you know it's time to transition. More than likely you're already taking some of the steps needed to move on with the next exciting stage in your life.

It's not ok to wait any longer. I've been speaking with dozens of boomer Owners about selling or transitioning their company and the same story is told to me over and over again.

'I can't do anything just yet. The time isn't right. I know I have to do something.'

The family members, and the many trusted advisers, Owners tend to surround themselves with tell me this story.

'I don't know what to tell my Dad/Mom or Client. We talk about selling or transitioning the business but he/she/they keep putting it off. I wish I knew what to say or do.'

Yes we all know you have a deep emotional attachment to the company you built. And yes 2008 was an unexpected blow. You've had at least 8 years to recover or not. It is unlikely the world will suddenly drop a 'selling gift' into your lap. So you have to reconcile dealing with the company and its' future now.

If you don't, the decision will be made for you. Health, the economy, competition or industry changes will dictate what happens next. At that point all bets are off. You've lost control and you didn't get into business just so you could give up control.

The first thing you need to know is you likely have an inflated opinion on the value of your company. Sorry, but that's the cold hard truth.

In addition, at least 80% of your wealth is likely tied up in your single largest asset - the business. The biggest sale you will ever make will be the business itself. Tell the truth, are you really prepared?

Your future, and the well being of many other people, depends on the steps you take over the next few years. You know you need to do something now or it might be too late. After all, it will likely take 3-5 years from start to finish to be fully out of the business.

Right now you may not know exactly what you'll do after the business is sold. That's part of the journey. How about we agree that time with family, good health and a little extended holiday is a great place to start.

When you started or took over the company did you really have all the answers? I didn't think so.

The clock is ticking, whether you're ready or not. Take the first step into your future now. I feel strongly about this because I know if you wait too long, we may end up with more closed businesses than our economy can absorb.

BUYERS and SELLERS

What Sellers Are Thinking

Buyers and Sellers see things differently. Buying or Selling a business raises many questions. This section will help each side understand the other a little better. The following is very top level and each buying and selling situation is very different. Nobody really has the upper hand. Each side has its' own set of challenges.

We've been getting a lot of calls recently from Buyers looking for good companies. If you've ever been on the buying side of the table, you know it can be incredibly frustrating. Inexperienced Sellers with companies not ready for sale, being represented by unqualified advisers and Owners actually trying to conduct a sale by themselves.

Unrealistic expectations of Sellers and often ridiculous time-frames are the norm. 'I need to sell in 90 days. And I need 10 x what the company is really worth. Can you do it?' It's not pretty, just pretty difficult for both sides.

On the other hand, Selling is a big step filled with questions, self-doubt and unreal pressure both self-imposed and from outside. Having someone on your side can be a huge relief.

Likely you are a first time Seller or the last company you sold was years ago. The learning curve for selling your business today is steep and this may have kept you from acting in the past. It can seem like you're working alone and in the dark. You have many questions and limited resources to find good quality answers.

You're entering a world you have previously not thought that much about. Now that it's here you're plain scared. The sale of your company is typically 80% about you and 20% the business. This is what's keeping you up at night.

1. What's my really company worth?
2. What will I do with myself after the sale?
3. What happens to my staff, customers and vendors?
4. When is the right time to sell?
5. How do I find the right Buyer for my business?

As a Seller you're looking to satisfy a few basic conditions to make this a successful experience. This is a major step and likely you will only take it once in your business life.

1. You must have the best price possible, because you've worked for years to build your company and you have real financial needs for the future.

2. You want as much cash at closing as you can get. Mostly because the promise of future rewards from earn outs is not guaranteed.

3. Some kind of promise that the company will continue to be successful and live on to prosper for a long time. Your good name will be untarnished.

4. Reassurances your employees, vendors, partners and customers will be treated fairly.

5. You want to be respected and treated well throughout the whole transition phase.

You want a fair deal where the Buyer does what they say they will do and on a schedule you both have agreed to.

What Buyers Are Thinking

Each Buyer has their own agenda and will have a different impact on the Seller. Getting there can be more work than they are prepared to take on internally, so different methods are employed. Going direct can be frustrating and very time consuming. So Buyers use Merger and Acquisition Firms, Business Brokers, and their own networks to identify and acquire target companies.

In a recent survey, Buyers of businesses were asked to identify the single biggest concern they had about purchasing a company. Overwhelmingly 75% said that finding the right business was key. Getting a good deal, arranging financing or not finding out certain issues before closing the deal were all important, but securing the right company was the key.

As a Buyer, it's pretty straight forward. They want to find the right fit, at the best price with the least amount of risk. Finding good companies to buy, can be like looking for a needle in a haystack.

The Buyer is looking for a few other things as well and likely more than the Seller is. After all the Buyer could be living with the results of the acquisition of your business for a very long time to come.

1. They do not want to find any surprises. No hidden debts, agreements or side deals.

2. The truth about your business. Honest financials, realistic forecasts, legitimate customer and vendor relationships.

3. Good value for their investment of time and money.

4. A return on their investment and a steady ongoing income.

5. Ability to payoff, in a reasonable amount of time, any debts the company may have incurred.

6. A business with the potential to grow without requiring more debt. However, aggressive experienced Buyers understand debt, when used properly, can be a legitimate part of growth.

7. A company that could be quickly integrated into their existing business or as part of a roll-up.

The experienced Buyer will look at the value of your company by dissecting these items and many more with a very fine microscope.

1. They will thoroughly review all past earnings reports. Especially the ones you don't want to show them.

2. The management team will be assessed individually and as a group. No, if they don't play nice now, they will not be able to fool the Buyer. So make sure you fix your team, now.

3. Are you diversified within your product or service offerings or are you a one trick pony?

4. What type of business are you in? Paint or a specific niche.

5. Is the industry growing, shrinking or evolving into something else? Where does your company fit within the changing industry?

6. Are your Sale Agreement terms well thought out and adhered to or out of date and ignored?

7. Are employees happy or sad, disruptive or cooperative, ready for new Owners or reluctant?

8. Is your competition aggressive or passively active?

9. Is it a good location where you operate and appropriate for where you sell?

10. Is your equipment paid for or leased, old needing repair/replacement, or new and up to date?

Buyers expect your business to have cash flow to cover these items and more.

1. Pay off corporate debt that has been accumulated by you.

2. Ability to pay the new Owner a reasonable salary.

3. Provide the Buyer with payment for a quick return of their down payment.

4. Funds as a safety cushion to help with the inevitable unexpected. And there will be something.

Buyers will expect your business to meet these criteria and many more to consider your business a viable opportunity.

1. All your current, detailed and complete Financials, Inventory, Sales and Tax Records are easily available.

2. A clean and efficient work place. Your workplace can be indicative of the rest of your company.

3. You have good, loyal, enthusiastic and reliable employees.

Challenges Buyers Face With Sellers

Granted Buyers see the situation a little one sided so, for Owners, take this section with a tiny grain of salt. Talk to a Buyer and they will recite sad story after sad story. The tale of the runaway Owner. The frustration a Buyer has when they know they have what the business needs to be way more profitable and the Owner who doesn't get it. The Owner flat out lies and thinks they'll not get caught. The list goes on. The Owner has outrageous expectations.

Here are a few typical situations that come up far more often than one might think. Ask yourself this. As a Seller, are you the good experience or the difficult one?

1. The Sellers' business is ready to expand nationally or even internationally, but requires funding, management, operations, sales and marketing help. But the Seller doesn't want to give up anything to get the help.

2. The Seller has mind blowing technology, (at least in their minds) and not enough funding or management skill. They've been chasing the technology brass ring for years. And they know it will hit any time now. So forget about buying them for anything less than some unreasonable number.

3. The established profitable business looking for a Buyer. However they have been advised that the company is worth far more than it is. Usually this advice comes from unqualified sources. Like the Owners fishing buddy accountant.

4. The Owner who needs a little sales and marketing help to jump 2 levels. Some operations and finance assistance wouldn't hurt either. They are solid, just underperforming, not really reaching the levels that could be achieved.

Unfortunately the Owner isn't willing to pay for help pre sale. They may also be a little afraid to grow and staying small is the comfort zone the Owner prefers. So the Buyer is turned away. The Owner may have missed an opportunity to dramatically increase the value of the company.

5. The lifestyle company that could be so much more. Stalled at a particular annual sales level well below its' potential. It simply provides the Owner with a nice lifestyle and all their needs met. That is until they realize it won't be enough for retirement. So the asking price is based on their personal requirements and not on the marketplace and what is reasonable. Buyers see this all the time in companies with annual sales under $3 million.

6. The Owner isn't sure about selling and may just leave the Buyer at the altar or keep making unreasonable demands until the Buyer just goes away. Meanwhile the Buyer is spending money on legal and accounting fees to qualify the company.

7. The classic I'm saving the business for my kids. So I can't sell it to you. Some day they will take it over. Call back in a few years and we'll see if it worked out.

8. I'll sell the company to you but you can't change anything from staff to products to the logo. You have to run it as is. Like that's going to happen.

Any of the above examples could be you, a BABO looking to transition. Sounding familiar? What are you going to do about it? Miss the opportunity you've been waiting for.

7 Main Types Of Buyers

1. Strategic Buyers

These tend to be companies growing via acquisition. They search for purchase targets aligned with their own offerings or providing complementary products and services.

Compatible culture and cost savings derived from being able to eliminate business function overlaps are viewed as bonuses. Sometimes this comes at a cost to you as redundant staff are at high risk of being let go. On the other hand superior staff could find themselves with better positions in the new merged company.

Your entire corporate identity can end up disappearing as the new owners absorb you completely into their world.

So if you're looking for an exit, where the future of your company, its' identity, as you created it, and your staff is a key concern you may want to avoid the Strategic Buyer.

2. Private Equity

Typically an investment vehicle for institutional investors or high net-worth individuals. Limited Partners invest their money into funds that General Partners of the firm use to buy companies. Usually targeting businesses within a specific industry.

The firms executives ideally maximize the growth of the companies, in their portfolio, over a five to seven year period. Then they move to your side of the desk selling the business(s), earning a return for the investors and themselves.

Private Equity executives contribute financial resources and corporate experience to help take your company to the next level. Sometimes this includes retaining you the owner /operator over an extended period of time beyond a traditional 18-36 month transition. Assuming you all get along, the new owners will benefit greatly from your years of experience, expertise, employee, vendor, and customer relationships.

This is a two way street if you'd prefer to retain a piece of your equity stake. Selling to a PE firm could prove to be the way you drive your business to its full potential and share financially in the success. They will more than likely make changes you don't agree with as they are usually looking to maximize the profits over the short term.

Additional owners equal more decision makers. Quite different from running your own business the way you want to. Board members can get in the way of innovative ideas. They can also help to avoid bad ones and bring good ones. They will likely be fixated on the bottom line.

3. Family Offices

While resembling private equity groups in some ways, they differ in other characteristics. Family offices invest the wealth of a single family. Often, but not always, focused on the industry where they made their fortune. The top priority is to make sure the wealth continues to grow over many future generations. They also understand the dynamic of a family run business, with all its' added challenges. In some cases they can bring solutions.

It's often the case where, over the years, less and less family members actually participate in the businesses they own. Compared with private equity firms, family offices usually hold less risky portfolios, investing over longer periods of time.

As with most high net worth people, family offices can operate well below the radar and be difficult to identify or reach. Introductions by mutual friends and business associates tend to be the communication method of the day. Mostly investing with cash not debt, they offer sale prices usually lower than other Buyers.

If you're fortunate you could sell to a family from within your own industry. The bonus of their connections, experience, industry guidance and financial assistance might help propel your business to incredible new heights. Beyond what you ever imagined. Or you simply cash out.

4. Holding Company, Buy and Hold

Sometimes called shell companies, exist to buy and own other companies. They don't operate, produce or sell any products or services. Instead, they generate revenue from the profits of the businesses they have an investment in or own outright. While everyone points to Warren Buffet as the classic example, there are many holding companies operating with interests in specific industries. Berkshire Hathaway has interests in a myriad of often disassociated companies.

Holding companies typically prefer a controlling interest in the companies they invest in or they simply own outright. They often have a hands off relationship. If you continue to be successful, that is. If you fit their criteria and pass the strict financial and management success standards it can be a good way to cash out.

As with PE firms, additional owners could mean extra decision makers. Could be a benefit or a hindrance.

5. Search Fund

Search funds consist typically of an individual operator or two. They're backed by a group of investors, looking to buy a business and take over running it. Investors don't always have the time to get involved in multiple companies other than on an advisory basis. They do however, have a need to make their money work for them. So the fund identifies an operator with a desire to run a company, a proven ability and the level of experience to successfully do it. The operators first task is to find an appropriate company to buy. The group then buys your company for the operator, confident they will generate a return. The operator earns shares of the company over time and after reaching agreed upon milestones usually tied into profit.

Typically the operator is committed to a long term relationship with the investors and the acquired company. The company gets an often younger, full time leader and a recharge of energy and ideas. A great way to take your business to the next level. You may get to see some of those ideas you put on the back burner actually realized.

6. Your Employees

You can sell to an outside party or look inside to your employees. Some Owners dream about a Buyer who comes in doesn't change anything and the company continues on as if you were still in charge. If that's your goal you might think an Employee-Stock Ownership Plan (ESOP) is the answer. Just remember there are no guarantees. New folks in charge will always have their own ideas of how things should run.

This methodology can be complicated and not every business has staff that want to accept the responsibility or have the skills necessary to be successful.

You need to bring in a specialist with ESOPs and discuss it openly and honestly with your staff. Just because you think it's a great idea doesn't mean they will.

There are government programs to assist with the process. Rules change by country, state or province. Might be good idea to find a champion within your own organization to do some of the initial leg work. If you can't find anyone to put in the work upfront, perhaps an ESOP is not a viable route for you.

7. Newbie Buyers

Lately I've been receiving calls from new Buyers. That is, a business person looking to buy a company. Traditional retirement isn't how they see their future and buying and running a company is one of the options on their list.

They may never have purchased or run a company before. Their previous experience includes senior management roles, running a department or even running the whole company. However they may not have, in recent years, run an entrepreneurial venture on their own.

In some cases they are looking to buy a job. Franchises used to fill the need. Now these folks are also considering the purchase of a company on the smaller side, often with under $3 million dollars in annual sales. Sometimes the appetite for an acquisition is far grander and they could be hunting for a $ 5-10 million company.

So they begin the long process of fact finding, networking and talking with lots of people about buying a business. The process can take years and be very frustrating. Particularly when they try buying a business directly from the Owner. As we have discussed earlier.

Each newbie Buyer I speak with immediately tells me about the business they tried to buy. How the Seller was difficult to deal with, unreasonable about price and in the end often left the Buyer at the altar. Recurring theme.

Earlier in the introduction I mentioned that this book was designed, in part, to help Buyers understand the depth of personal challenge the Seller is going through. So Buyers, keep reading and give it another try. This time you might have a bit of an edge as you'll, at the very least, have an appreciation for what the Seller is thinking and more importantly feeling. Try sitting on their side of the desk.

As A Seller You Come In Two Flavours

Most Owners are first time Sellers like yourself. If you've done any research into selling, you know there's a world of landmines waiting for you. Even for the savviest Owner, obstacles to a successful sale are wide and deep. You need to be honest with yourself, to know who you are and how you will be perceived.

Your natural instinct is to be cautious about new relationships, while keeping your guard up. This includes working with advisers, Buyers and providers of professional services. Eventually you get to know each other and a flow develops between you. The difference with this situation vs other business relationships is that a sale or transition is for all the marbles and you're playing the game for the first time

Regardless of whether you're a Seller at ease or one under pressure. The experience, for most of you, is like walking in the dark in your own house. You know where things are supposed to be, but it's still somewhat unknown.

Here's a tip for Buyers and advisers. Tread lightly or you could spook a Seller. They're torn between wanting to work with you and running away. There is a lot going on in their heads and you need to respect that.

Are You A Peaceful Seller?

1. You're incredibly proud of your company. Both profitable and still growing. You talk about it to anyone who will listen. You've put your heart and soul into it and are justifiably proud. As you should be. Building a successful business is a great accomplishment.

2. Some of you ask for or take every dollar you can, all the way through the transaction. After all, that's what you've been

doing for years. There's a good reason the company is so profitable and you have done well.

3. Your due diligence documents, are up to date, accurate and provided quickly. The documents are thorough and usually offer more than what was asked for.

4. You've always stayed away from lawsuits you can't win. The last thing you want is a lawsuit after closing. Clean operations and acquisitions are the norm for you.

5. Buyers can expect a smooth transition and likely a long term relationship with you long after the closing. All the potential good anticipated from this kind of Seller requires the Buyer be equally reasonable in their actions.

6. Good employees usually stay with the company post closing. Assuming they are treated fairly. You may be relaxed but your employees may not be.

7. Here's a tip. Sometimes employees are happy with the status quo and when change is thrust upon them they react by fleeing. This is not your fault. It could be they will experience great changes that would make their lives much better. Doesn't matter, change is not always welcome. So don't be surprised when one of your staff says they are leaving. They simply like it the way it is and that's it.

8. Your bigger customers are happy and continue adding sales to their accounts throughout the transition.

9. As a proud Seller you will go above and beyond to share, with the Buyer, best practises learned over the years in your industry. Secrets to maintaining great customer and vendor relationships are freely offered. You want the new Owners to be as successful as possible.

Are You Selling While Under Loads Of Pressure?

1. As a desperate Seller you tend to have flat or declining sales. One profitable division or product line. Only 20% of your customers represent 80% of sales. Financials are inaccurate. You may have an unrelated company attached to the main company but not part of the sale. Do you have one or all of the above?

2. You're very stressed and living with a bad situation that only seems to worsen the longer you wait. The company has been slipping for months and likely years. You know something should have been done about it but you didn't want to admit failure to yourself. Now it's too late and you're desperate, operating at a personal low. You think you can fool the Buyer with false accounting and half truths about staff, customers and vendors. Maybe some Buyers, but not all.

3. The due diligence reports you were asked for take a long time to generate and are incomplete. The list of reasons specific information cannot be provided just keeps growing until you hear yourself say the dog ate it.

4. As you are not a desirable business to buy, it becomes clear to you that most of the folks involved with the company including employees, investors and vendors will be losers in the transaction, if there is one. You also come to the realization the only winners will be the Buyers who acquire whatever is salvageable for a bargain price. You can divert your resentment towards the Buyers and blame them for your troubles. You will likely tell the staff it's the Buyers fault not yours. The staff know the truth.

5. Some inexperienced Buyers, especially those responsible for investing 'OPM' other people's money, get excited about investigating and bidding on a distressed company. They can be blinded by the deal and want nothing less than to

complete a transaction. As a desperate Seller you may look for the naive Buyer, almost like a predator and will exploit them the same way.

6. Your desperate and borderline fraudulent behavior peaks before an actual bankruptcy. You reach out for a final move to save the company. Or raise cash to repay existing investors or yourself. You believe it's the responsibility of the Buyer and their trusted advisers to detect an inevitable bankruptcy. If the financial statements are a misrepresentation of the real situation the business implosion might not be obvious to a newbie or even an experienced Buyer.

7. When the transaction is complete, the Buyer could find themselves with only the slow paying, low margin customers. Unproductive employees who drive the company deeper into trouble. Angry vendors turning up and an unwarranted negative reputation is created. Potentially existing but, as yet, unidentified lenders and law suits appear. The Buyer has lost their savings and or the investors money.

As a Seller you need to recognize who you are and how you appear to a Buyer. It may be time for an attitude change.

As a Buyer you get what you pay for. If you're honest with yourself you will have seen it coming. Even though you just don't want to admit it to yourself. Open eyes on both sides are required.

You Have A $ Number You Need To Sell For

Much like selling a home, you get a number in your head and that's what you need to sell. But where did it come from? Here are a few questions you should ask yourself before moving forward. Working off an unrealistic premise could result in wasted weeks or months.

Answer these questions honestly because you want to be dealing with a real world value for your company. Avoid disappointment.

1. Where did you get the number from? Was it from a reliable source? Someone who knows what they're talking about.

2. Does the source have experience with selling businesses?

3. What is your number based on? Consistent sales, the intangible goodwill, or the potential you know the company has? Or is it just what you need?

4. Do you really think someone is willing to pay what you want?

5. Are you being realistic about what your needs are? Most of us are, at least in some way, preparing for retirement. Experts have provided formulas and estimates of what we need to retire comfortably. But I believe no one really knows what will happen, in the future, to your health or that of a loved one, the economy, or any one of a number of factors that can adversely affect your well being.

6. Does your number take into consideration other issues like your employees? Are you planning on sharing the wealth with long term, loyal employees?

7. What if you can't find a Buyer to match your number?

8. Will you get professional help to arrive at a realistic value for your company? Keep it real and you'll be less frustrated with the offers, if and when they come.

The Why In The Equation

Buyers want to know why you do what you do. They know what you do, but not why. They also want to know why you're selling. It's a way to get closer to you and can influence their decision on buying your company. To a certain extent they're buying you and the business.

On the surface it may sound like a simple question, but what they are really asking is what motivates you to drive this business? Is it to make money? Or to bring a valuable solution to the marketplace.

At some point, prior to purchase, Buyers will talk to your management and likely some of your staff. Have you thought about how your employees will answer these and many other questions?

1. Why do you do what you do?
2. Why do you work here?
3. Why do you think you're important to the company?
4. Why do you think you're not important?
5. Will you stay after the transition and why?
6. Why do you think the Owner is selling?
7. Does the company have any unexploited opportunities?

I Want To Be Irrelevant, And So Should You

I'm working very hard to build WarrenBDC into something great and make myself irrelevant in the process. The strategy is a simple:

1. Have a big vision and, make it worthy of your time and effort.

2. Bring great people with varied skill sets and experiences onboard. Make sure they speak their mind.

3. Let them do what they do best and are most passionate about. We all have a superpower and at our core we know what it is. This is usually accompanied by a deep desire to unleash it to its' fullest potential.

4. Create a desirable inclusive atmosphere, great people want to be a part of.

If I succeed, they will thrive and likely take the company much further than I ever could on my own.

So what does irrelevant mean to me? Right now and for the foreseeable future I will maintain the vision and lead the charge. As we grow I'll slowly replace my superpowers with others who demonstrate the same abilities and let them take over.

At some point I will become redundant, irrelevant and unnecessary to managing and growing the business. I will then have succeeded.

You should also strive for irrelevance so the business operates without you. This is a key factor when Buyers are considering purchasing your business.

It's not easy and requires some real grit on your part. While many day to day functional activities are taken care of by staff there are still top level decisions that always seem to fall into your lap. No this is not by fluke it is by design, your design. The desire to be relevant and important to the process.

There is a reason that some of you have kept your business running at a particular sales level for years. It's not always because opportunities have dried up. Nor is it the new developments within your industry. It's because there is a comfort in working in a particular sized business. You found your comfort zone and staying there is well, more comfortable.

I know it sounds counterintuitive since you spent the last few decades making most of the key decisions, creating and massaging the vision, leading the sales and generally driving the business to its' current success.

It won't be easy to give up the responsibilities and let go. But the Owner who has done this typically finds that among the many factors used by Buyers to make a purchase decision, this one is key.

Put yourself in the Buyers seat. You do the transaction and suddenly you get hit by a bus. There is a falling out and you refuse to continue the transition relationship. You don't agree with a change they're making and your instinct is to fight it or worse sabotage the change. If the Buyer is dependent upon one or two people to determine the fate of the business post sale, they're highly unlikely to move forward with a purchase.

You can say it won't happen all you want, but when one is dealing with real money and time invested in the success of a venture they want all the right cards in their hand.

So become irrelevant personally, to the point where you become incredibly desirable as a company.

YOU MIGHT BE FEELING THIS WAY

You're Ready When You're Ready

How do you know when it's time to get serious about transitioning? No two Owners are alike and no two situations are the same. Circumstances may be similar at a higher level, but we all have our own specific challenges.

Before you're really committed to a transition, you'll go through stuff, they'll be all kinds of things to address. No shortage for sure. Family issues - ailing parent, things that have to be dealt with in the office - replacing staff, personal social commitments - daughter's wedding and the list goes on. There will always be other things you need to do but if you just keep letting those things get in your way you're never ever going to get to where you really need to be so you can just sit down and start working on your future.

It's 80% about what's going on inside your head. You deciding what you need to do. You choosing where you want to be. You selecting how you want to live the balance of your life. Let's not forget the other significant factor in your decision making, your spouse. Regardless of whether they are involved with the day to day running of the business or not, their opinion matters. A lot. Just ask them.

It's 20% about the company. Figuring out what needs to be done for the business and finding the resources. There is some work involved but really it's not that complex. It's certainly not as complicated as you determining what you want your life to look like in the next 5, 10, 20 or 30 years.

Being clear and comfortable with your decisions. This is truly what you want to do to construct your ideal transition. Your future life should be based around what your true desires are.

Don't forget the people closest to you. Family, partners, and employees. You'll also have to take into consideration what they want/expect or need.

I know an Owner who sold his company and helped all his key employees get settled into their next phase of life. He provided them with advice and financial assistance to start a business.

Whether you're working with a team of professionals or not, second thoughts can creep into your thinking and hamper your progress. Owners have been known to change their minds mid stream about selling. Maybe you want to give your kids a chance to run or buy the business. Or you become re-energized about the company, believing you can make it even more valuable on your own. Then there is the possibility that you find the whole preparation process just too much and dying with your boots on seems way easier.

It never stops until you are finally transitioned out. Or does it? There will be countless conversations with yourself and others about your decisions on price, the Buyer, your role after the sale etc. Expect to keep second guessing yourself regardless of how well it went. Doesn't mean you did badly, it's just our nature to keep rehashing the big 'what if'.

Work Life Balance

We've spent enough of the book on work. The life part is about how you spend your time when you're not working. It's also about who you spend your time with. Family, friends, the ones who you can't wait to see and the others you are not keen to. As Johnny Cash once said. 'Son, I don't know you well enough to miss you.'

Spouse, children and grandchildren are at the top of the list. As the old story goes, when asked on their deathbed. What was your biggest regret? Most people say the same thing. Wish I had spent more time with my family. In fact, I hear that now from clients about grandchildren. I didn't spend enough time with my kids while they were growing up. But I won't let that happen with my grandchildren.

As with many Owners, you may not want to stop working altogether. After all, you're still healthy and work is exciting, enriching, satisfying and fulfilling. All I'm suggesting is you think about balance between working and living. Balance usually comes down to time. I know you love what you do. But maybe those closest to you love to be with you.

You May Already Be In Change Mode

If any of these activities are happening in your life, then you're already changing. Each one by themselves could be perceived as a simple lone action. But when added up, you see the big picture.

1. You're reviewing your current will. If your lawyer hasn't suggested this they should. Don't forget the personal will and the business will.

2. Taking a hard look at your personal finances. No one really knows what they'll need for retirement. There are formulas and expert opinions but you really don't know how long you'll live or what will happen along the way. So plan for the worst and hope for the best.

3. You've been planning to take longer vacations in the near future or you may have already started taking some.

4. Getting in shape, working with a personal trainer or at least walking more.

5. Downsizing your home and maybe even downsizing your business. Outsourcing functions you used to do internally.

6. Handing off all your responsibilities within the company, day to day and long term planning.

7. Managing the affairs/care of an aging parent.

8. Attending graduation of and or marrying off your youngest child. A proud moment and a real jolt of reality. You are moving on. Like it or not.

9. Re-purposing the extra bedroom for your home office or as a hobby room.

10. Investigating locations for a winter home. Buying a place.

11. Thinking about the future of the company and possibly your role changing.

12. Add your own._____

It's been a good run and you accomplished quite a bit with the company, but it's time to let go. Get on with your life. I know I hear it all the time, you don't know what you'll do if you sell or transition. You also don't know what you're missing.

Are You Running Out Of Runway?

Feeling tired and not prepared to do any more work on the business? Maybe you waited too long to sell and the end is still not in sight. The kids are now older and not interested in running the company. Employees are not prepared to buy or run the business. You may have had an inquiry to purchase in the past, but that's long gone. Although you still think it could happen, it's highly unlikely.

You're being advised to run things differently so you can attract Buyers. It's apparent to you and everyone else, you can't or don't want to run your company differently. It's worked well for 30 years.

It really is time to sell and you don't have 5 years to do it. Now what? Can you sell it sooner? That remains to be seen. Even if you could, it's likely you won't get anywhere near what you want or need.

Pressured and no idea who to turn to? Giving it away or just closing down won't pay for your retirement. Like many other BABOs, you never saw this coming and now unfortunately, you really don't know what you're going to do. The pressure is building and it's not nice.

If you're running out of runway, then perhaps you should be looking into and thinking about the many options that could be available.

For some it's going to be a tough go selling and retiring comfortably. For others you and your family may be covered for now but what if (insert your worst fear here)?

Right now the best thing you can do is to keep reading.

Taking The First Step In Transitioning

Why is taking the first step so difficult? You had to do it on the first day of school, living away from home the first time, and when you started dating. Somehow you made it through to the other side.

Anxiety, looking for help and over thinking were all part of the paralyzing experiences. You imagined all the things that could go wrong and eventually saw the wonderful outcomes that were realized when it went right and the pieces fell into place.

So why do we continue to freeze up? Or choose to do nothing when the opportunity for change is presented. It can come either as an option or is thrust upon us with no choice. The result could be bad and you will learn from it to try again or good and the experience will be something wonderful.

As I look back, I realize that many of my best life experiences came from having no place to retreat to and only one path to follow; the road to going forward and finding my future.

You did it a few decades ago when the idea of starting or taking over your business first popped into your head. I'll bet it worked out better than you ever imagined. Yes of course there were challenges. But what a ride.

I Just Deleted Someone From My Database

You never know when it's your time. I received a call the other day that threw me for a loop. A reader, of my weekly emails, that I've known over the years suddenly passed away. He was younger than me, fit, friendly and outgoing. At the top of his game.

His sister called to inform me, as she had been going over his emails and came across my most recent weekly email. Not really knowing our relationship, she thought I should know he passed. I wished her family my condolences and said he was a good man.

I didn't know GS well, only to exchange the odd email and have an occasional call. We supported each other with an electronic pat on the back and a 'we'll do something together some day' promise.

He was a good man, hard working, honest, good at his job, and absolutely someone I would have recommended. I wish I had known him better. As for doing something together, that ship has sailed.

I deleted his name from my database as I wouldn't want to cause unnecessary grief, in the future, to his family with an unexpected accidental email. Too little too late.

As busy as we are, you never know when it's your time. Something to think about.

Are You 'Running On Empty'

A great song by Jackson Browne. Unfortunately I can only use the title and artists' name.

The meaning of the lyrics didn't hit me until I read it the second time. Your company is like the closest relationship you've ever had. It may have run its' course, for you. Much the way a personal relationship dies out.

Put the book down, go online, find the song Running On Empty and listen to it. At least twice. It's worth the break and serves as a little bit different approach to your thinking.

Playing With Your Grandchildren Enough?

Ok maybe not the type of question you would expect in a book about buying and selling companies, but just as important as any other.

I ask this question all the time just to see if the Seller is thinking about priorities beyond business stuff. Taking the grandchildren to school, on trips around the world and generally getting to know them as people and influencing their lives is extremely rewarding for both of you. If you don't make the time now, it will slip away far too quickly. The opportunity doesn't come around very often and when it does you need to jump on it.

Nobody is suggesting you sell the company and devote all your time to them. Just think about easing back on business activities and making room for the best time in your life.

As boomers, we all say this with tongue in cheek. My grandchildren are way more fun than their parents. Why couldn't we just have the grandchildren. No we don't mean it, but it is an interesting thought.

YOU NEED TO DO THIS FOR YOU

Decide What You Want?

'If you don't know where you are going, any road will get you there.'
Lewis Carroll

At this stage in your life you have many choices, but the big question is what do you want? Sometimes the obvious is not the real answer. The old party line for retirement was playing golf, traveling and spending time with family. Maybe doing some volunteer or charity work.

All great ideas, unfortunately they quickly get old and sooner than later you will become restless and frustrated. You crave an identifiable place in society, a position that was formerly taken up by being the Owner of your company.

You have lived a life that likely revolved around your business and the thrill, the buzz that came from the ups and inevitable downs of running a company. A steady stream of successes and overcoming failures is a difficult drug to give up and hard to live without. So what do you do now? How do you replace the excitement of running a business?

Most Owners do take some time to play golf, sail, travel etc. and then start to think about what they really want to do. I'm suggesting you begin the process now. Figure out now what you want to do after the sale and transition.

Believe it or not, the hardest part of selling or transitioning out of your business is the emotional roller coaster you'll ride. But the feeling you get when it's over is well worth it.

One of the key questions will be - What will I do when I leave?

Standing In The Way Of Your Happiness?

You know what the next step is, but if you're like many people there's something holding you back. You can't put your finger on it. Maybe it's fear of failure or simply not knowing what will happen.

For many of us this unsaid, unwritten and often imaginary thing stops us from moving forward. We miss out on what could be, because we are afraid of what might happen.

I'm declaring today 'Next Step Day'. Please pick one thing you've been stalled on about selling your business and take the next step today. Let me know how it turns out.

When Complacency Misses Opportunity

You might be asking yourself how did I get here? Sometimes we get comfortable with our lives and a routine becomes, well you know, routine. You don't think about it, you just do it. Other things come up and there is never a shortage of distractions to grab your attention.

But ask yourself at what cost? Are you missing out on a great opportunity? Personal or business, it doesn't matter. Do we get complacent and miss accomplishing something greater with larger potential impact on our lives and those closest to us? Is there a cost to being complacent?

You likely have a short list of things you'd like to do or business opportunities you could take advantage of but you don't.

So here is the challenge. Pick one personal item and one business thought on your list. Write out the next steps and clearly state the reward. Read and reread the first step until you realize how simple it is to take it. Then get started.

Get others involved and once the ideas are on their way, go back to the lists and pick some more. The secret is to engage others in the process. They can encourage you and or do the work. As long as you take action in the first place.

This is for your own good. It doesn't matter if we're talking about a company, a job, a habit or a friendship. If you don't take the first step and pull your head out of the sand you will never get to where you really want to be. Just take one small, first step and savour the sweetness. Don't worry about the rest, it will all fall into place.

Change Yourself, Change The Business

Change can be frightening and debilitating or enriching and energizing. One thing we've learned from working with many business founders and Owners is that change impacts your life and the lives of your employees, as much as the company.

There is something called Kaizen. Chinese and Japanese for 'continuous improvement'. When used in the business sense and applied to the workplace, Kaizen refers to activities that continually improve all functions and involve all employees from the CEO to the assembly line workers.

Change usually comes from the top down. If you haven't personally taken up this activity to improve your business you might want to get going on it. The benefits can be wide and deep for you, your staff and the company.

Now introduce Kaizen thinking to your teams. Staff suggestions that are acted upon and prove to make jobs easier or more productive, customers happier and the company more successful are rewarding emotionally for them. Ideally you'll make it monetarily for them too.

The staff will be energized by seeing and experiencing positive changes. Your company will run better. Prospective Buyers will view this attitude as a huge asset. It starts with you from the top and flows down and throughout the company.

Be On The Same Page As Your Spouse

We're so busy running our business, often we don't make time to find out if we're still on the same page as those closest to us. Decisions we make today will absolutely impact our future and the lives of those nearest to us. Spouse, partner, family, and work family are all affected by the choices we make.

Let's start with our spouse or significant other. Usually when I ask an Owner if they know how their spouse would like to spend the next 5, 10 or 15 years they look at me like I'm nuts. You may be doing this right now. Then there is that moment of realization and the answer becomes 'not really'. Again, you may be saying this now.

So here is what I suggest. Tonight, crack open a bottle of wine. Ask your spouse how they want to spend the next 15 years. This is not about you, so don't offer up your plans. The first part of the conversation is only about your spouse. Listen and listen some more.

Once they're finished, clarify their ideas so you're both on the same page. Now add your own plans into the conversation and have a true two-way conversation. You did it when you first became serious about each other. I'll bet it worked out well.

When the subject of the business comes up and it will, you'll both have many questions. How valuable is it and how sellable is it? This is when you need to start the process of assembling a team of trusted advisers who have experience in buying and selling companies.

Being Married Makes You A Better Entrepreneur

Entrepreneurs often apply their life skills to running and growing the business. Here are some lessons that work equally in a marriage as they do in your business life. A supportive successful marriage can offer many lessons for the business Owner to apply at the office.

1. **Communication.** It's key, whether with your staff or your spouse. Do it often and do it consistently. Make it positive regardless of the message.

2. **Plan ahead.** In marriage, you plan for retirement and the years ahead. Any business should be planning for the short term - 12 months, midterm - next three years and long term - the future. And you should have backup plans.

3. **Respect.** In a marriage it might be as simple as 'thank you for making dinner', it's not always about buying expensive gifts. In business it could be so many things. Sometimes all people want is to be appreciated and you likely have dozens of opportunities every day to do this.

4. **Compromise.** Like in a marriage, business is a partnership with all the staff. There's negotiation and sometimes conflicting opinions. Learn to bend when it's important; stand firm when necessary. You need to truly understand the nature of compromise and practise it often.

5. **Happiness.** Everybody has to be a winner; it has to be win-win. That's similar to marriage. You need to work to understand what a win means. That doesn't have to mean a loss for someone else. You have to look for what they want, and it's not always what you might think. Your partner or staff might not want more money. It just might be they want more time off or more responsibility.

6. **Criticism.** Constructive criticism is good, but there has to be a balance between criticism and compliments. Good criticism is done in the spirit of helping somebody do something better; personal or professional. Criticism should not be thrown around; rather, criticism is used when it's truly important. Staff morale and productivity will suffer when they feel negativity. A critique of your work can be deflating even if it is done constructively. Whether it's your spouse or staff, never criticize publicly - it will do more harm than good. And it should not be done in anger. Tonality and timing are important.

Thank You For Making Money

Some business Owners want to grow their company while others don't. I understand the degree of desired growth varying from Owner to Owner or even partner to partner. What I don't get are the reasons some of you use for not growing at all or even trying.

Sometimes I'll ask a business Owner, contemplating selling their company, this question. Would you prefer to sell your current company or one twice the size? Assume, in both cases, they are equally profitable. The answer is not always predictable.

I've heard several negative answers from 'I'm happy coasting' to 'we can't handle any more sales'. 'More sales mean more problems.' 'I don't need any more money.' And the one that drives me crazy - money is evil. Or at least it makes you a bad person if you have money. This one came from the spouse.

There is nothing wrong with making money. However, if that was your only goal to accumulate wealth, then I might agree with the critics. It's all about what you do with it.

So here is one of my thoughts on the subject of philanthropy. Ask yourself this. How much good could I do if I doubled the profitability of my business prior to selling?

In other words, what could I do to improve the world with the surplus funds that would come from selling a bigger more profitable business.

Instead of coasting, selling low or giving the business away I could take my years of experience and expertise in making widgets and turbo-charge the company over the next few years.

Then leave on a high, do some good and change people's lives forever with the additional funds. Family, friends, business associates or strangers it doesn't really matter who you help.

The boomer generation has had a massive impact on society, both good and bad. I'd like to believe we can leave a legacy of having left the world in a much better place. Sounds pretty good to me.

Ignorance Is Not Bliss, Living Your Dream Is

As discussed earlier in the book, there is a highly disproportionate number of you - BABOs, who will not take the first step in determining the future of your company. You would rather let a few more years roll by than start the process. Tic toc time is running out.

On the subject of selling/transitioning out of your business, there are 5 things I can assure you of:

1. It will take much longer than you had ever thought. Try 3-5 years.

2. You can't do it successfully without the right team. Likely you don't have that team right now.

3. There is so much to know. You don't know what you don't know. The process is filled with potholes and surprises.

4. The lineup of Sellers is getting longer. Right now you're at the back of the line. And some of you are not even in the room.

5. To put it off any longer will only result in either getting less than you think the company is worth or simply closing the door and receiving nothing. You need a plan. You may end up somewhere else when done, but you need a plan to succeed.

Let's Talk About Procrastin...

Yes I had to do it. Whether it's you or your partner or both, procrastination can be a killer. What it does to you and your business, employees etc. can be significantly damaging to your potential for sale.

Procrastination can come from fear of what might happen - good or bad, a gut feeling that now is not the right time, other peoples advice or agendas and a myriad of other places. The point is that not moving forward usually has a price. Sometimes it saves you from a big mistake other times it keeps you from achieving a goal.

So what is it this week that you're behind on or is keeping you from taking a first step toward transition? What decision are you not moving forward with? What is really holding you back? You know what they say, recognizing you have a problem is the first step in solving it. If you can't figure it out on your own then get some help.

Work Less and Accomplish More

Ever feel like your efforts are not achieving the results you'd like? Working harder is not always the answer. We get so many irons in the fire we forget to pull the hot ones out. Overwhelm sets in and then everything suffers. We ignore the 80/20 rule, where 20% of the work usually delivers 80% of the reward. Check your accounting records, 20% of your products or services are 80% of your sales. Lead with these and the others will follow.

What we also don't do is keep the top 20% of our customers really happy. Many of us unfortunately spend too much time looking for new customers and forget the good ones we already have.

Find more of the 20% type of customer and spend less time trying to land and service the 80% customer. This is a significantly better use of your time. Just make sure you don't end with only a few 20% type clients that control your destiny.

Sometimes working less delivers better results. I've been practicing what I preach and the results are amazing. I'm seeing more quality opportunities come together easier and enjoying my life much more. You can too! Focus on the important stuff vs hiding inside the rest. It's easy to get caught in the details and lose sight of the goal.

Thinking time vs reacting time is key. The old expression measure twice and cut once is actually true. This includes thinking outside the box, looking at it from a different angle and getting someone else's perspective through fresh eyes. You're sure to see other better ways to tackle a challenge or reach a goal.

Work on what you're passionate about. That's when nothing can stop you. Do the stuff you like to do and it's not work. Spend your free time enjoying family and friends, volunteer work, philanthropy or quietly thinking about the next move.

YOU NEED TO DO THIS FOR THE BUSINESS

Partners, Can't Always Live With Them

Couldn't really have done it without them. Whatever you think about your partner now, they did make a contribution and it's better to focus on the good over the bad.

While every situation is a little different, some long term business relationships are better than others. But then comes the time to end this 'marriage' of sorts and move into the next phase of your lives.

Unfortunately you want to sell and your partner doesn't. Or it's the other way around. Doesn't really matter. What's important is you have a somewhat difficult sea to navigate. This is going to be unlike any other business decision you and your partner have ever had to make before. You want to maintain your friendship but business is business and you have your family to think about. Not to mention your responsibility to loyal employees, vendors and the many customers you've served and have supported you over the years.

So do you go it alone, plan to work the transition out between yourselves and risk the business, your relationship and perhaps your future well being? Or do you bring in experienced experts to help steer the ship so you both get to your respective destinations with minimal disruption to your business and your personal lives? It's up to you.

Ask a few friends who have gone through this. Read a few books on the subject. In the end it doesn't really matter how much you read or what your friends say. If you don't have the right team to help plan and execute, it's all just interesting reading and conversation.

Be On The Same Page As Your Partner(s)

Sound familiar? This is very much like the situation with your spouse and the same thinking applies. So I will repeat myself a little.

We're so busy running our business, often we don't make the time to find out if we're still on the same page as our partner(s). Decisions made today will absolutely impact our collective future.

Let's look at your partner(s). Usually when I ask an Owner if they know how their partner would like to spend the next 5, 10 or 15 years they look at me like I'm nuts. Then there is that moment of realization and the answer becomes 'not really' or we've been meaning to have that conversation.

So here is what I suggest. Today, leave the office, and go out for lunch or dinner with your partner(s). Then ask how they want to spend the next 15 years. This is not about you, so do not offer up your plans. The first part of the conversation is only about your partner(s). Listen, listen and listen some more.

Once they're finished, clarify their thoughts so you're all clear. Now add your own plans into the conversation.

You did it when you first started working with each other. Yes of course you had/have challenges. But you're still together.

Naturally the first question will likely be. Do you want to stay? Followed by what is the value of the company? You need the help of professionals to answer the second question.

Get The Best Out Of Everyone

When you sell or transition you need to make sure your successor understands the value of getting the best from everyone and you need to help them. They might be a family member, a long time employee or an outside acquirer. In any case you want the new Owners to have as much success as possible. Particularly if part of your compensation is tied into the future financial achievement of the company.

The new management may have been groomed to run the family business, in some cases, for their entire adult lives. Or you may decide to offer a loyal employee or management team member that opportunity. The originators of the business often try for years to educate, share their experiences, impart their wisdom, and mould their successors. Some succeed others don't. Family isn't always the best choice. In fact it's more rare than you might think.

Share what made you successful and make sure that goes for everyone involved with the company as well. Give the new Owners complete and unfettered access to you and the senior management team. An immediate and never ending inside edge to the key goings on of the organization.

Some of the same benefits (experience, familiarity, and loyalty) can be gained from non-family, non-management employees and business associates who offer expertise and experiences that are different from yours. They may not be an Owner but what they offer is invaluable. Make sure you pass this insight and access on to the new management.

In some cases the new generation will continue to operate the business as it had been run in the past, a safe short-term measure.

This strategy may have worked for the previous generation, but circumstances are changing at a dramatic pace. We are living in a time of new technology, new needs, and new ways of approaching problems. E-commerce, database marketing, social media, big box and online stores, branding, and many other new terms have not only entered our small business vocabulary, they have taken business over.

As part of the older management you may be set in your ways, a little tired, and perhaps a little too comfortable with a particular style of conducting business that has provided you with years of triumph (usually tempered by a few bumps in the road).

The younger management may be full of energy and have new ideas for reinventing the business. But working together, you both need to blend the best of both generations. Preserve the successes from the past, incorporate the new opportunities, and build for the future.

A reminder to the older generation: not everything old is good nor is everything new bad.

To the younger generation remember: not everything old is bad nor is everything new good.

Revisit The Back Burner

As an Owner, we have all accumulated new or crazy ideas that have not been implemented. Some came from customer requests, an offhand conversation with an employee or supplier, middle of the night brainstorms and strategic planning sessions you only partially executed.

We all have them, just never could find the time to do anything about them. Tried once, had some success but you weren't comfortable with the amount of work required to fully exploit the idea. So you just left it on the back burner to simmer or worse, get cold.

I guarantee if there was an idea generated and not acted upon, it wouldn't take long to quickly determine if it could have a life. You want to know if there is an ember of possibility or not. Blow on the ember and massive flames can grow out of it. If the idea proves to not be viable then use it as a starting point. One idea typically begets another and another etc.

Are you sitting on other unexploited sales, money left on the table? An opportunity to take your tired business in a different direction. You could be sitting on a pot of gold. And if you aren't prepared to take the idea to the next step, then pretty it up and use it to sweeten the deal for a prospective Buyer.

Once you dust them off, be careful as you may now want to move forward on some of the ideas and put the sale on the back burner. My suggestion is to continue preparing for the sale as you never know when the right Buyer will come along or you no longer have the choice about selling.

Where Would You Be Without Customers?

Customers are the most important component of your selling offer. You can have the best product or service and the most knowledgeable and impressive staff, but without happy customers, you may have no one interested in buying your company.

Having no sales will lead to fewer staff or at best, a less-qualified staff, leading to a downward spiral. This situation may sound like a doom and gloom prediction, but a solution is not far out of your reach.

In fact, there are many steps you can take to not only secure your relationship with existing customers but also attract and retain new ones. The old adage 'treat customers as you wish to be treated' has never been more relevant. Competition is fierce and small companies are stealing business from formidable competitors through solid, reliable customer service. The stigma of small companies being too small to handle customer needs is disappearing.

If you're executing a growth through acquisition strategy to get your sales up prior to selling, you need great customer relationship processes in place first.

Great customer service can even the playing field with larger or better financed competitors. It can make all the difference in the world to the success of your business and a successful sale.

The Elephant In The Boardroom

It's not uncommon for a family business to have an outstanding issue or individual that we might refer to as the 'elephant in the room'. We all know who they are and what needs to be done. But still, year after year goes by and the company suffers. And so do the employees.

Yes sometimes it is you, the Owner. But you can't pile every problem on your shoulders. It could be a spouse (involved or uninvolved) who interferes with the business. A partner not seeing eye to eye with you or even willing to consider your view. An employee in a key position not doing their job. A next generation or any age family member with too much power but not enough experience. A failure to keep up with your industry, a competitor running right past you, a part timer hired to perform an important function but not delivering, the list goes on and on.

The worst part is you know in your head what the problem is but your heart won't let you solve it. Whatever or whomever the issue is that's keeping your company from further success needs to be on the table, sooner rather than later. Because later will likely be too late.

Outside resources can usually help to resolve the issue cleaner and faster so you can move forward with more ease. And yes if you could solve it internally, why haven't you? Whomever you call, do it right now! You'll thank me. In all likelihood the 'elephant' will be relieved, because typically they know they are the problem.

A Buyer will find out sooner or later and they may not be as forgiving as you. If you really care about the problem employee, deal with it now for their sake and yours.

Getting Your Ducks In Row

What do you do when someone lets you down? Hey, stuff happens and people (associates, employees, suppliers, customers, family or friends) can fail to deliver. When they miss a deadline, it's not always their fault. Could be their associate let them down, illness, or just mother nature/the universe messing with you. But did you get a call or email saying there was a problem?

Is it consistent, do they let you down over and over again? Is it something different each time? Maybe they don't care about you or are they driving you away consciously or subconsciously?

In any case you need to find out. In my experience 'If it looks like a duck, and walks like a duck...it's likely a duck.' Yes there are exceptions. Not often though.

Assuming it's a duck, you have two clear choices.

1. Do nothing, get upset, let them keep disappointing you until you blow up or worse blow up a relationship with them or an innocent third party.
2. Cut them loose. Better for you and better for them.

Because it's NOT ok for you and really not good when the Buyer gets into the due diligence phase. They will look under every rock and open every closed door to find out what is wrong and determine what it might take to fix. Bigger problems mean more work, possible expense and reason to not proceed. So cleaning up your mess before is extremely important.

We All Need Guides And Cheerleaders

It's our year end and as usual, as the Owner, I've taken some much needed time to stop and reflect on what we, at WarrenBDC, have accomplished and where we are going. You may have the same experience about your life and business at your year end.

I know what needs to be checked off next and clearly am aware there is work to do. So as I'm sure you can imagine, there are equal amounts of excitement and overwhelm floating through my mind. You may be feeling the same emotions with your company or in your personal life.

Motivation could be wanting personal growth to get more out of life or company expansion to enjoy the benefits of being larger or to eventually transition out. If you're reading this book it's likely thinking about the immediate future and the prospect of selling.

Simply saying just buckle down and do it is not always as easy it sounds. The real answer is to engage others to work with you. We all need guides, cheerleaders and those who help with the actual work.

If you're feeling overwhelmed with your situation, as many BABOs are, and would like some new friends who get it, we'd like to join your team for a few minutes in a quick conversation or perhaps a few years for a deeper relationship. There I did it that's my plug.

12 Tips For Increasing Your Company Value

As I've said earlier it's all about the value of the company, how it's presented and the desirability to a Buyer. Here are some tips to help you get started on increasing value, long before you put it on the market for sale. This is a team exercise not a solo project.

1. Seek objective, outside, experienced professional help. If you try to prepare the company for sale yourself, you will likely take your eye off the day-to-day running of the business, cause unnecessary anxiety, and either keep your business where it is or hurt it. Diminishing the value.

2. Now is a great time to rethink your business. Think again about your current customers, competition, industry changes, and technology. Even rethink the type of business you're in. Many successful businesses have managed to stay successful by moving with the times. They saw that the needs of their customers were changing and acted on it.

3. Assess your company's current status, across all departments. Put everything on the table, both the good and the bad. Include areas of the business you are proud of and problems you wish would just go away. Address issues relating to staff, products and services, location, finance, profitability, and new business development.

4. Keep some, change some. Determine what your customers like about you and what they would like to see changed. Be honest with yourself. Talk to your customers.

5. Maintain objectivity, emotion has no place in this process. To achieve a successful assessment, you must do what is best for your company. This may mean letting long-term employees go or finding new suppliers, dropping products/services and creating new ones.

6. Review the past looking carefully at all your efforts, successes and failures. If you're running a program or department but cannot justify its expense with increased profitability, productivity or sales, consider cancelling it or placing it on hold.

7. Review competitive activity often. A new entry in a market will use new sales and marketing techniques or follow new thinking to achieve sales that you didn't know were possible.

8. Take time to review existing staff closely. Do they fit in with your growth or sale plans. Companies moving toward success have been thwarted by staff who didn't agree with the new ways or were afraid the company would succeed. The last person you expect to come forward will be the first to go.

9. Be flexible and prepared to adjust your transition plan as new opportunities and challenges arise.

10. Perseverance is an absolute must. If you give up too early, you may fall short of the transition you desire.

11. Speed is essential in preparing a company for sale. Take advantage of every day, to improve your value, as you don't know when the Buyer will show up.

12. Be careful and quiet. Your competitors may have heard you are thinking about selling and could take advantage moving in on your customers. Initially you should just tell staff, suppliers or customers you're just growing the company.

Working With A Team Successfully

As discussed earlier in this book you will require a team of experienced professionals to help plan and execute a successful exit. They must have experience with buying and selling businesses. There are many situations to be faced and decisions to be made that will require a different solution for a transition vs a normal business as usual scenario.

1. Be careful not to get swayed too far from the original vision while remaining open to new ideas. The benefit of a team approach is to provide insights and viewpoints different from yours. The downside is becoming overwhelmed by all the new ideas. You could forget the original motives, objectives, and strategies. Don't become so overwhelmed you decide to do nothing. Or run off in too many directions.

2. Listen to your own internal resources. Sometimes, as an Owner, you assume you only require an outside source. Your internal team is invaluable in providing up to date information about operations, finance, sales, marketing, customers, products, and services. They're close to the purchaser and the end user. They possess first-hand daily knowledge of product use, demand for services, and old and new customer profiles are often there just for the asking.

   They're able to advise you on internal resources such as finance, and the development of and capacity to handle special sales, increased demand for services, and order processing. Any changes you are considering need to be run by the people with day to day responsibility.

3. The external team you gather around you is equally important. To be effective, members of an external team must bring with them buying and selling experience, a good understanding of your business and a clear appreciation of

timing. The external team can provide ideas that are outside the day-to-day life of your company. They bring fresh eyes and an objectivity not found within an internal team.

4. Don't assume the external resource is automatically correct. Rightly or wrongly, you may find yourself more open to ideas from an outside resource than your own staff. Don't jump blindly into the new ideas just because they're from an outsider. Challenge the information and check with the internal team for their views. Make sure the external source can contribute information you do not already know.

5. Integrate all resources you bring in. Your external team may be assembled from more than one company. It may be necessary to integrate this collection of individuals and instill a true team spirit.

6. Avoid ego justification. Don't fall victim to NIH (not invented here). Many solid ideas never make it past the investigation stage because an Owner didn't think of it. Be open to new ideas and study them.

7. Your idea may not be the best one. The opposite of NIH (not invented here), but equally destructive, is IHMBR (invented here, must be right). Some people go from idea straight to execution and nothing will sway them from this path. These are the Owners who will by any means and at any cost do it their way. They are usually the same small business Owners who jump from one supplier to another. They often move for the wrong reasons.

8. Check with others for objective, educated, and reliable opinions. You're looking for more than a 'What do you think?' opinion. Asking someone what they think without first identifying objectives or strategy is like opening 'Pandora's Box.' You will receive personal opinions based on their limited experience. You risk abandoning a potentially logical and valuable approach for the wrong reasons.

9. If you're making changes, don't expect results right away. Running a business and preparing for transition is a constantly changing set of circumstances. Your company changes internally, competitors are unpredictable and customer needs evolve.

10. If it sounds too good, it likely is. Be wary of the transition adviser who claims to have the power to solve all your problems instantly. Transitioning is ultimately your job. The team may change and you will get stronger with experience.

11. Make sure all departments and aspects of your business are covered. If you use an outside resource, have a representative from the company participate (have them sign an NDA or substitute a trustworthy adviser). There should not be new issues uncovered after decisions are made simply because you didn't know.

Avoid Common Business Selling Mistakes

Owners make mistakes when selling their businesses and end up paying a price. It doesn't matter how successful you are in your industry, how many advisers are on your team or how savvy a business person you are. Selling can be fraught with unexpected actions by you, Buyers, their advisers or in fact your advisers.

Not to forget all the noise going on in your head as you contemplate and action the end of something that has been at the core of your life for decades.

Some mistakes to avoid and ideas on what to do.

1. You haven't taken the time to sit down and really figure out who you are, what you want next and why you want it. Time for serious soul searching.

2. The company you've built may be successful but it's not desirable by Buyers. Look in the mirror. Now take action.

3. You have not prepared yourself, the staff, or your company for a successful transition. It's never too late.

4. You haven't assembled a team of experienced advisers to help with the sale and transition. Start with one or interview many. Advisers will have others to bring to you.

5. You may not have considered what you owe to the employees and investors - if any. Look inside yourself.

6. You have not assessed the Buyer's true intentions and what they plan for the future of your company, once it is no longer 'your company'. Just ask them.

7. You have little knowledge of what to expect pre sale, during the process or post sale after the deal has been completed.

YOUR FUTURE

Share Your Profits, Knowledge And Experience

In many lifestyle businesses the Owner typically keeps the company a certain size because you're comfortable with managing only so much. Life is good, staff are fairly compensated and so it goes from year to year. You've created a machine but only driven it so far. This operating style has worked well over time for many Owners.

It's Like you own a Ferrari and have been driving it to the store for milk. You can do so much more with the business machine you created. It's a crime not to. Then again you already knew that.

Suggestion #1 Maximize the Company

Grow what you have. Share all your knowledge, experience and resources with your internal and external teams and get the company to where you have multiple choices for your future. Steer the business to a point where it runs well and without you. Stay working full or part time. Sell on your terms if and when you want. I guarantee, if you do this, you will learn a lot about yourself and those around you.

Suggestion #2 Grow Just a Little More

Make just 10% more profit and give it away. If you think you don't need the additional funds then share your extra profit with staff or philanthropic endeavours. It's good for the recipients and great for you. CAUTION When you realize how easy it is to add 10% and share it, you may want to go further.

Suggestion #3 Give Back To Your Current Team.

Share all your knowledge and experience with staff and organize an employee buyout. Pick a successor from your current team. If that is not reasonable, bring someone in from outside to support your staff. Identify a leader with a desire to carry on your legacy, work with your team and grow the company to the next level.

Suggestion #4 Share Outside Your Company

Go outside your existing business and share money, knowledge and experience. It's all valuable. Continue on this path after you sell or transition. It doesn't have to stop. If it's in you to share it's with you for life.

Consider Buying Your Competitors

Forward thinking business Owners are doing 'roll-ups'. Growing by acquisition, buying up the local competition or complementary companies.

They know the trend is for larger Buyers to acquire profitable, more substantial companies. So it makes sense to give them what they're looking for.

If you do the roll-up and integration into your company for them, the Buyer can come along a little later and acquire the whole package. No muss no fuss. You get to offer Buyers a much larger and more desirable company to purchase. Making your exit easier and more profitable for you. Selling a company under $10 million in annual sales will likely get you 3-4 x EBITDA. Over $10 million and you could realize 6+ x EBITDA.

You know your competition and already have a relationship with them. In many cases they're in the same age range as you and also have a requirement for an exit strategy.

It's like starting out with a bunch of great baseball cards, part of a set. You go out to your friends and accumulate the rest and create a complete set. Then you sell the whole thing to a collector. The sum of the parts is more valuable than the individual pieces.

Do not try this on your own. In order to do it right, you will most definitely need help with the whole acquisition, integration and growing part of the plan.

NEXT STEPS

Forget About Selling Your Business

No I don't mean that literally. Focus on the positive, increasing the value of your company. Not the negative of leaving your comfort zone. If you do it right you'll have options. If you change your mind you'll have a better business. Either way it's a win win for you.

9 Review Tips For Creating Options and Making Sure You Exit Well

1. Not sure where to start, get a qualified team. Engage experts in operations, finance, sales & marketing, human resources, legal and wealth management. Make sure they understand what is needed to exit a business successfully.

2. You need to be irrelevant. Stop working in the business and start working on the business. Pull away from the day to day responsibilities and spend quality time looking at the present and future of your industry and your business.

3. Only do what you love to do. Get back in touch with why you loved building your company. Re-energize yourself and enjoy the journey. You won't feel as pressured and wind up making the wrong deal.

4. Fix the broken stuff. People, systems, finance etc. Often it is the unwillingness of you the Owner to make the tough decisions that will be your downfall. If it walks like a duck and talks like a duck it won't fix itself, or it would have already.

5. Get your sales and marketing updated and aligned. Make sure they're working in an integrated effort. Good sales and marketing are key to your success.

6. It's not just about great sales numbers. Great operations and strong financial controls deliver profitability and desirability as well.

7. Add at least 4-5 years on to your exit strategy. After you make the company desirable you need to find a Buyer. Count on another year to do the deal and 3 more to ease your way out. The new Owners will likely require your participation to provide experience, industry introductions, continuity with staff, vendors, and customers.

8. Not sure when you want to exit? Run improvement efforts parallel to the process, as you don't know how long it will take and you just may change your mind.

9. Create options. It's not always black or white, selling or closing. Sometimes you just need to develop options. There are many ways to structure a deal. Talk to experts.

A Final Thought

Selling or transitioning your business is a big step, both personally and professionally. Surround yourself with good people. Make a plan and anticipate there will be changes all the way through the process.

You will experience many highs and lows, much like you have for the last few decades while running your company. So nothing new. Look at it this way. You've been training for this next step in your life for years.

ABOUT THE AUTHOR

Eric Gilboord Biography

- Eric has worked with hundreds of Small and Medium-sized Business Owners over the past 22 years. For the last 3 years he's worked exclusively with Boomer Aged Business Owners.

- He is a management consultant, speaker, the author of several books, a columnist and the creator of hundreds of articles, seen in national newspapers and magazines, online and read regularly via his weekly emails.

- His first book 'Just Tell Me What To Do - Easy Marketing Tips for Small Business' was a best seller. The new 2016 updated Second Edition 'Just Tell Me More - Marketing Tips In 10 Minute Chunks' was just released. He also co-authored a book called Marketing Masters.

- Eric speaks to groups of Small and Medium-sized Business Owners on growing and preparing their businesses for sale. The goal is to increase the value of their company in order to sell on their terms and for more. He also speaks to Trusted Advisers to help them better understand BABOs.

- Three years ago he transitioned his marketing services company to WarrenBDC. Focused on helping Boomer Aged Business Owners prepare their company for sale by increasing the value, pre sale. WarrenBDC also helps Buyers acquire and then post sale, grow the business.

Contact Info:
Eric Gilboord eric@ericgilboord.com www.ericgilboord.com
WarrenBDC eric@warrenbdc.com www.warrenbdc.com
Warren Business Development Center Inc.

www.ingramcontent.com/pod-product-compliance
Lightning Source LLC
Chambersburg PA
CBHW060622210326
41520CB00010B/1442

* 9 7 8 0 9 8 6 8 9 3 2 4 7 *